The Crown You Never Lost

The Crown You Never Lost

Pamela Blaney

Copyright © 2025 by Pamela Blaney

All rights reserved. No part of this book may be reproduced in any manner whatsoever without written permission except in the case of brief quotations embodied in critical articles and reviews.

First Printing, 2025

For every woman who thought she had lost her crown...

You never lost It.

Contents

Dedication ... v

1. HEARTBREAK WHISPERS LIES ... 4
2. THE WEIGHT OF EXPECTATIONS ... 19
3. SHATTERED MIRRORS ... 42
4. PICKING UP THE PIECES ... 50
5. THE CROWN OF FREEDOM ... 59
6. THE CROWN WITHIN ... 68
7. THE POWER OF DETACHMENT ... 76
8. QUIET LUXURY OF THE SOUL ... 87
9. REBUILDING SELF ... 93
10. ABUNDANCE UNFOLDING ... 107
11. THE CROWN WAS ALWAYS YOURS ... 114
12. A MESSAGE FROM PAMELA ... 118

About the Author ... 121

YOU NEVER LOST IT

There was a night when I stood in front of the bathroom mirror, gripping the edge of the sink as though it might hold me together. My phone still glowed on the counter; the words etched across the screen:

"I'm sorry, but I'm just not in it anymore."

They weren't cruel, but they were final. And in the silence that followed, I felt stripped bare.

I stared at my reflection and barely recognised her. My face was swollen from tears, my eyes dull and hollow. I thought: This is what it looks like to lose yourself. This is what it feels like to be empty.

But here's the truth I couldn't see then: I hadn't lost myself. My worth wasn't shattered on the tiles, and my dignity hadn't walked out the door with him. My crown - the invisible mark of my value, my identity, my strength - had never been taken. It had only slipped, waiting for me to lift my head and place it back where it belonged.

This book is about that crown. About the part of you that remains even when life feels broken. You don't have to earn it, prove it, or chase it. You cannot lose it, no matter how undone you feel. At worst, it tilts. At times, it feels unbearably heavy. Sometimes it hides beneath the weight of grief or expectation. But it never leaves.

This is a story of remembering. My story, yes - but also a guide for your own. An invitation to lift your head, steady your crown, and see yourself again as the woman you have always been: Whole, Radiant, Worthy.

"The sharpest blade that heartbreak carries
is the lie of not enough."

It doesn't arrive all at once.
It slips into the mind in many tongues,
disguising itself as reason, as logic, as self-awareness.

But it is none of those things.
It is poison, and I drank it slowly.

If I had been taller, funnier, more successful –
he would have stayed.

If I hadn't made that mistake.
If only I'd said the right thing.
He would have chosen me –
if only I had been enough.

If I'd given him more,
loved harder,
held on tighter,
things would be different.
He would still love me.

And in those early days,
I believed every version of that lie.

I bled beneath it.

1

HEARTBREAK WHISPERS LIES

There was a night I will never forget. It is etched into me the way some moments carve themselves so deeply into memory that no amount of time can erode them. I was standing in my bathroom, the mirror harsh in its fluorescent light, my reflection blurred by tears that refused to stop spilling, hot and unrelenting.

My phone lay on the counter, its screen still glowing, the final message glaring at me as though it wanted to sear itself into my skin:

"I'm sorry but I'm just not in it anymore".

His words weren't cruel, not exactly. They weren't violent or loud. But they were short. Final. Unyielding. And because they came as plain black text on a glowing white screen, they carried an iciness no spoken word ever could. There was no tone to interpret, no softness to misread. Just flat certainty.

The words hit harder than any argument ever had. Not because they were laced with anger, but because they were so final. So clean. So absolute. They left no space for negotiation, no window for hope. They didn't even leave a crack where reconciliation might slip in. They closed the door and locked it.

I gripped the edge of the sink with both hands, white-knuckled, the porcelain cold and unyielding beneath my skin. My body trembled - not with rage, but with the kind of grief that hollows you out in a single instant. I could hear the rush of blood in my ears, feel my breath stutter and catch as though even my body didn't know how to continue without him.

The mirror reflected a stranger. My eyes were swollen, rimmed red, lashes clumped with tears. My cheeks were blotched and damp, my lips pressed so tightly together they were almost bloodless. I leaned closer, staring, searching, desperate to find the woman I had been only hours before - as though she might still be hiding somewhere behind the puffiness and despair.

But all I saw was absence. I whispered aloud, my voice trembling, so faint it felt foreign in the stillness: "Who am I now? What do I have left?" The final word cracked in my throat and splintered into the silence like glass shattering.

The bathroom felt cavernous and claustrophobic all at once. The fluorescent light buzzed above me, unforgiving, spotlighting every flaw in my skin, every crack in my composure. The phone screen dimmed, then went black, leaving me alone with nothing but my own reflection and the echo of words that had dismantled me.

It was as if my crown - that invisible symbol of my worth - had shattered. The identity I had so carefully built, the confidence I had once carried with ease, seemed to lie in fragments on the cold bathroom tiles. I felt dethroned. Small. Unworthy. As if my power had been stripped from me in the space of a single sentence.

And in that moment, I believed the lie heartbreak tells most convincingly: that everything I was depended on being chosen. And now that I wasn't, I was nothing at all.

THE SILENCE THAT FOLLOWED

The hours after that message passed in a haze. I drifted through my home like a shadow, unable to focus, unable to sit still, too heavy to move. Every sound felt amplified - the hum of the refrigerator, the ticking of the clock, the faint rush of cars passing outside. But inside, there was nothing. Just silence.

Silence has a weight to it. It doesn't just hang in the air; it presses in. It curls into your chest, fills your throat, settles into your stomach until you feel sick with it.

I wanted him to call. To send another message. To explain, to backtrack, to take it back. I stared at my phone, waiting, begging it to light up. But it didn't.

Instead, the silence wrapped itself around me like a shroud. And into that silence came the whispers.

Heartbreak doesn't need volume. It doesn't roar. It doesn't need to. It seeps in through the cracks when you're most vulnerable, soft and insidious, wearing the mask of truth.

You weren't enough.

If you had been prettier, funnier, more successful, he would have stayed. If you hadn't made that mistake, he wouldn't have left.

If you had given more, loved harder, held on tighter, things would be different.

The lies multiplied, each one sharper than the last, until they crowded my mind so thickly, I couldn't see past them.

I tried to argue back. I reminded myself of the times he had said he loved me, the life we had shared. But the lies were louder.

They pressed against me until I began to believe them.

THE SPIRAL

I remember one night, sitting in my car, parked in the driveway but unable to go inside. The summer air was heavy and still, but I shivered. The dashboard lights glowed faintly, casting the interior in a dull amber haze. I gripped the steering wheel with both hands, staring into nothing, while my mind replayed every conversation, every look, every word, searching for the exact point where it had all gone wrong.

I thought of the things I had said and the things I hadn't. The moments I had been too tired, too distracted, too human. My mind twisted them into proof:

See? That's why he left. That's why you weren't enough.

I became a detective in my own life, gathering evidence against myself, building a case that heartbreak had already judged and sentenced. The harder I tried to find answers, the deeper I fell into the spiral.

And maybe you've been there too. Maybe you've sat in your car, or on the edge of your bed, or in the middle of a crowded room, your mind spinning with questions that never resolve. Maybe you've felt that desperate need to explain the unexplainable, to make sense of someone else's choice by turning the blame inward.

That's the cruelty of heartbreak. It doesn't just take away the person you love. It makes you doubt the very ground you stand on.

WHY HEARTBREAK FEELS LIKE LOSS OF SELF

For weeks afterwards, I moved through the world convinced everyone could see it too. That strangers in the supermarket, colleagues at work, friends at dinner could somehow detect that my crown had slipped. I imagined them looking at me differently - not as whole, not as radiant, but as broken. Abandoned. Less-than.

But here is the truth I would come to learn, though not quickly and not easily: the crown had never left. The loss I believed was total was only an illusion. Heartbreak had convinced me of lies, but the essence of who I was remained untouched, waiting for me to remember. This is the illusion of loss - the story heartbreak tells when we are too raw, too bruised, too tender to see clearly.

Heartbreak is rarely about just one thing. It isn't only the absence of a person, or the silence where their voice used to be. It is the collapse of the identity we tethered to their presence. When we love deeply, we don't only give affection, time, or energy - we give meaning. Their attention becomes proof that we are valuable. Their approval becomes evidence that we are enough. Their love becomes the mirror through which we measure ourselves. So when they leave, the loss cuts deeper than companionship. It severs the reflection we relied on to confirm our worth. And without it, the questions come fast and brutal:

Am I still loveable? Am I still desirable? Am I still whole?

This is where the illusion of loss begins. Because the truth - though invisible in those raw early days - is that our worth was never tied to their gaze. Our crown does not vanish when their eyes turn away. And yet heartbreak convinces us otherwise.

The illusion burrows into daily life until even ordinary moments feel altered. Sleep becomes restless. Food turns tasteless. Music is unbearable. Colours dull, as though the world itself has dimmed in sympathy with your grief. Everything echoes the absence, and in that fog, it is easy to believe your very essence has gone with them.

But pain is not proof of loss. Pain is only fog. And when it clears - even faintly, even for a moment - you begin to see that the crown has been there all along, waiting for you to remember.

THE LIE OF "NOT ENOUGH"

The sharpest blade heartbreak carries is the lie of not enough.

It doesn't arrive all at once. It slips into the mind in many tongues, disguising itself as reason, as logic, as self-awareness. But it is none of those things. It is poison, and I drank it slowly.

If I had been taller, funnier, more successful - he would have stayed.

If I hadn't made that mistake. If only I'd said the right thing. He would have chosen me - if only I had been enough.

If I'd given him more, loved harder, held on tighter, things would be different. He would still love me. And in those early days, I believed every version of that lie.

I bled beneath it.

I remember nights lying awake, dissecting conversations word by word, as though the right phrase could rewind time and undo what had been done. I played the scene of me leaving like a movie reel on repeat, each time editing myself - smiling differently, speaking more softly, being somehow better. And I remember the comparisons. Scrolling through her photos, measuring myself against her body, her smile, her laugh, as if her existence erased my own. As if her being chosen meant I was disposable.

But here's the truth I could not see then: when someone leaves, it says everything about them and nothing about your worth. Their decision is about their readiness, their desires, their path. It is not a verdict on your value.

The crown doesn't vanish because they fail to see it. Their blindness is not your deficiency.

The lie of "not enough" is persuasive, yes. It wears many faces. But at its core, it is still only a lie. And once you name it as such, it begins to lose its power.

HOW WE ACT WHEN WE BELIEVE THE ILLUSION

When we believe the crown has slipped, we live as though it has.

We lower our heads - literally and figuratively. We stop meeting people's eyes. We shrink in spaces where we once stood tall. We second-guess our laughter, our opinions, our dreams, afraid of being too much, convinced that less of us will somehow be more acceptable.

We settle.

For jobs that drain us.

For relationships that erode us.

For friendships that do not celebrate us.

We accept crumbs of affection, convinced that crumbs are all we deserve.

I did this too. I learned how to disappear in plain sight. I stayed silent when I wanted to speak. I wore clothes that didn't feel like me, thinking maybe if I blended in, no one would notice the fracture lines. I agreed to plans I didn't want, smiled when I wanted to cry, nodded when I wanted to scream. I moulded myself into the shape I thought others would find palatable, because I believed my crown had been lost and I had to earn it back.

But crowns are not earned. They are not handed out as rewards for perfect behaviour or endless sacrifice. They are not given or taken by anyone else. They are claimed.

When we forget this, the cost is steep. We hand away our power piece by piece, waiting for someone else to restore it, to place the crown back on our head. But no one else can do that.

That choice belongs to us alone.

And when we finally remember this - when we dare to lift our heads again, even shakily, even with swollen eyes and trembling hands - that is when we begin to feel the weight of the crown returning. Not as something foreign or new, but as something that was always ours.

A FRIEND'S STORY

A friend once told me that after her eight-year relationship ended, she felt like a ghost of herself. She described standing in front of her wardrobe one morning and realising she had no idea what to wear - not because she lacked clothes, but because she didn't know her own taste anymore. For years, she had dressed to please him. Every colour, every cut, every style had been chosen with his approval in mind. Without him, she was lost. Tears streamed down her face and she told me, it's not because she missed him, but because she didn't recognise herself.

That moment became her turning point. She began buying clothes she liked, experimenting with styles she'd never dared to before. She cut her hair the way she'd secretly wanted for years. She began to see herself again, piece by piece.

Her story showed me something: the illusion of loss is also an invitation. An invitation to rebuild identity from the inside out, to wear the crown that is truly yours - not the crown someone else demanded.

POINT CARTWRIGHT - MY SAFE PLACE

There is a place I have always gone when the weight of the world feels unbearable: Malkana Crescent. It has always been more than just an address. It was the place that made me feel whole, the place where love felt certain, and where safety wrapped itself around me like a second skin. Even now, just driving past the old house somehow makes me feel whole, as though the memory of safety still lingers within its walls. The windows, the driveway, even the curve of the garden bed carry an echo of belonging. It reminds me that certain places hold you long after you've left them, as if the walls themselves remember.

Just up the road from Malkana Crescent, there is a lighthouse.

At this point in my life, the lighthouse at Point Cartwright had become that same kind of refuge. It stood there, tall and unwavering, watching over the sea and sky like it always had - a constant in a world where everything else felt like it was slipping away.

To reach it, you must climb a steep, winding path that coils its way up the hill, until the ocean spreads wide beneath you and the white tower rises behind you like a sentinel. Standing there, you can feel both small and infinite at the same time. The sea is relentless, unbroken, ancient. And the lighthouse - solid, steadfast - seems to whisper its quiet promise: you are safe here.

That evening, I needed its strength more than ever. The sun was sinking low, spilling its colours across the horizon - orange melting into pink, pink dissolving into violet. The air was heavy with salt, sharp and cleansing, the kind that clings to your skin and fills your lungs until you feel both raw and renewed. Below, the ocean thundered against the rocks, waves shattering into white spray, the sound so fierce it felt like the heartbeat of the earth itself.

Beside the lighthouse, there is a small clearing that feels like mine. My secret place, though I know others have sat there too, claiming it for their own. I brushed the branches aside, careful on the steep path, and lowered myself onto the weathered bench near the cliff's edge. From there, the sea stretched endlessly before me, swallowing the last light of the day. Behind me, the white tower stood tall against the bruised sky, a steadfast guardian.

I opened my notebook without planning to.

My hands moved almost on their own, as if they had been waiting for this moment.

Words poured out, jagged and raw:

I am not enough. I am replaceable. I am broken.

I am too much and not enough at the same time.

I froze. My chest tightened, my throat ached. Each sentence stared back at me like an accusation, pressing against me like stones stacked one on top of another. I couldn't look away. I was afraid that if I did, the words might leap from the page and cement themselves into me forever.

And then it happened.

A wave struck the rocks below with such force that the spray leapt high, cool droplets stinging my face. The sound cracked through the air - fierce, unrelenting, undeniable. In that instant, it was as if the ocean itself had risen to meet my pain, to answer the lies on the page. Its voice was wordless yet certain, roaring back:

No. This is not who you are!

Everything stilled. The sky, the sea, even my breath. And in that pause, something inside me shifted. It was faint, but unmistakable - like a thread pulling taut, like a crown straightening ever so slightly on my head. The crown I thought was shattered had not vanished at all. It had only tilted, waiting for me to lift my head.

I sat there for a long time, the wind biting at my skin, the notebook open in my lap. For the first time in months, I didn't feel completely lost. I felt a spark - tiny, flickering, fragile, but real.

A reminder that my crown had never left me.

THE ILLUSION OF LOSS

When I look back on that night at the lighthouse, I see now that nothing truly ended there. What ended was the illusion. The illusion that my worth depended on another person's choice. The illusion that loves leaving meant I was unlovable. The illusion that my crown had shattered.

That is the cruelty of heartbreak: it convinces you that the essence of who you are has been stolen, when it has only been hidden - buried beneath grief, expectation, and lies whispered too often to ignore.

But here is the truth I couldn't see then: the crown was never lost.

The crown had never left me. And it has never left you.

At times, it tilts. At times, it feels unbearably heavy. Sometimes it slips beneath the weight of loss, rejection, or the crushing demands of who others tell you to be. But it never disappears. The illusion of loss is powerful, yes. But it is only an illusion.

That night by the sea, I didn't walk away completely healed. I didn't stride down the hill wearing my crown perfectly straight. I walked away fragile, uncertain, and raw. But I also walked away with something I hadn't felt in months: the faintest spark of remembering. And remembering is where healing begins.

In the days that followed, I noticed how many crowns I had been wearing that were never mine to begin with. Crowns shaped by society's perceived standards. Crowns moulded by relationships. Crowns pressed down by the weight of human expectations. Some glittered, but they cut into my skin. Others were so heavy I could barely breathe beneath them. Heartbreak hadn't just convinced me I had lost my crown - it revealed that for years, I had been carrying the wrong ones. And that is where the real work began.

PRACTICES FOR RECLAIMING YOUR CROWN

Morning Grounding:

Place a hand on your heart before the day begins and whisper:

"My crown is steady. My worth is whole. My life is mine."

Mirror Work:

Meet your own eyes in the mirror and say:

"I am enough. I am crowned with dignity and worth."

Journalling the Illusion:

- Write down the lie's heartbreak tells you.
- Then write the truth beside each one.
- Keep the page where you can return to it often.

Crown Visualisation:

1. Close your eyes and imagine a glowing crown resting above your head. Lower it gently into place.

2. Feel its weight, not as a burden, but as presence.

"The only crown that frees you is the one you choose, because freedom doesn't come from being everything to everyone.

Freedom comes from choosing yourself."

2

THE WEIGHT OF EXPECTATIONS

After the night at the lighthouse, something in me shifted. I had seen through the illusion. I realised that my crown was never gone, only forgotten. For the first time in months, I felt a sliver of peace, a reminder that I was still whole.

But what I didn't expect was that, even as I began to remember my crown, it still felt unbearably heavy.

This was a different kind of weight. It wasn't the sharp sting of heartbreak anymore, but the slow, grinding pressure of expectations - the roles, duties, and unspoken rules that seemed to dictate who I was supposed to be.

I realised then that even before the breakup, I had been carrying crowns that weren't mine. Crowns moulded by my family's hopes. Crowns shaped by my partner's

preferences. Crowns forged in my children's expectations. Crowns demanded by society's standards.

Each one pressed down on me, leaving dents in my spirit. And the hardest truth of all? I had worn them for so long that I couldn't even tell which crown was truly mine anymore.

A FRIENDS STORY

A friend once told me about a man she had briefly dated. At first, he was all charm and warmth, the kind of person who knew how to make someone feel noticed. She said he made her feel safe, secure, seen.

But then the cracks began to show. A sudden distance. Little silences that seemed louder than words. In time, the truth surfaced: he already had a partner - she was simply away.

What hurt my friend the most wasn't only the betrayal, but the way he let her believe she mattered, even while knowing she was standing in borrowed space. He never admitted it. He just faded into silence, leaving her with questions that were never hers to carry.

She told me later the silence was worse than the truth would have been. Silence and lies only leave you debating with yourself. And that is its quiet cruelty - it strips clarity and leaves only confusion.

THE CROWNS WE NEVER CHOSE

That story stayed with me, because it showed how easily we accept crowns that were never ours. My friend wore the crown of his silence, heavy with doubt and dismissal, even though it had nothing to do with her worth.

We rarely notice the moment it begins - the slow placing of crowns that aren't ours: a raised eyebrow, a casual comment, the subtle pull of a cultural script. One crown becomes two, then three, and before long the weight feels normal.

We forget what it was like to move freely, to feel light, to wear only the crown that belongs to us.

Some of these crown's sparkle, catching the light in ways that make others admire them. "She's so reliable." "She's the perfect wife." "She's the kind of mother we all look up to." On the outside, they glitter. But inside, they cut into us like glass.

Others don't sparkle at all. They are heavy, unremarkable, plain iron. Yet we carry them because we think we must, because setting them down feels dangerous, selfish, or impossible.

I see it now: those crowns never made me whole. They only made me tired.

THE INVISIBLE RULES

Be a good girl. Don't be too much.

Don't speak too loudly.

Good girls are seen, not heard.

Work hard, but don't let your success make anyone uncomfortable.

Be kind, but not too bold. Achieve, but stay humble.

There's always someone worse off than you - which feels like your pain doesn't matter.

And never forget that pain is beauty.

These weren't rules anyone wrote down for me. They weren't spoken outright, not really. But somewhere along the way, I absorbed them. I believed this was how a "good girl" was supposed to live.

And because I picked them up so young, they felt like truth. They became the quiet script in my head, the crown I didn't even realise I was already wearing.

So I smiled politely when I wanted to shout.

I kept my achievements small so no one else would feel overshadowed.

I swallowed my pain, because I thought other people's struggles meant mine didn't matter. And I ignored my body's cries for rest,

because I believed beauty was supposed to hurt.

For me, the first crown was forged in childhood - not placed on my head by one person, but shaped by the world around me. Society means well at times, but its version of love often comes tangled with conditions. The rules were subtle, never spoken outright, but I absorbed them all the same.

They lived in small moments - in the way approval came when I was helpful, or how praise followed obedience, or how silence lingered after I expressed something that didn't fit the mould. I learned early to read between the lines: be a good girl, don't be difficult, work hard but don't make others uncomfortable, be kind but not too loud, achieve but stay humble.

They were absorbed through glances, comments,

stories, and the subtle shaping of everyday life. And slowly, without realising it, they became the measure of how I thought I had to exist in the world.

They became the invisible crown I wore - glittering on the outside, unbearably heavy underneath.

As a girl, I wore that crown eagerly. Being dependable made me feel loved. Taking responsibility brought approval. Approval became the currency of belonging, and I spent my whole life earning it.

But what I didn't realise then was the quiet bargain I was making: dim your light, and you will be safe. Stay small, and you will be loved.

THE PARTNER'S CROWN

The second crown I carried was shaped within love, or at least what I believed love required of me.

It didn't happen all at once, and it wasn't tied to any single partner. It was more like a quiet pattern that I slipped into without even realising it. At first, the adjustments seemed harmless: laughing a little softer so I didn't take up too much space, holding back my opinions in case they came across as "too much," choosing clothes I thought were flattering to someone else's taste instead of mine.

I even coloured my natural brown hair blonde, convincing myself I'd fit in better. Or perhaps because I thought it pleased him. I told myself these were normal compromises, the kind of adjustments love asked for. "Isn't that what a relationship is?" I reasoned. "Meeting in the middle, bending, blending, smoothing the edges?"

But the small adjustments began to add up.

I caught myself pretending not to know things I did, because somewhere inside I had absorbed a belief that a woman couldn't be both beautiful and intelligent. I convinced myself that if I showed my whole self, my wit, my sharpness, my fire. I would be too much. Too opinionated. Too intimidating. Too threatening.

And so, I began to enforce a quieter version of myself. That's the thing I see clearly now: no one told me directly to shrink. No one sat me down and said, don't speak. Don't shine. Don't be fully you. These weren't rules handed down as ultimatums, they were whispers, absorbed from the world around me, but carried out by me. I was the one who enforced them. I was the one who dimmed the light, convinced it was the only way to be loved.

I remember one night. We were surrounded by people I didn't know well, the room humming with conversation. A story sparked in me, something I wanted to share. A piece of myself that felt alive, and ready to connect. I opened my mouth to speak, and then... I stopped.

A voice inside hissed: Don't. Don't be too loud. Don't risk being judged. Smile, laugh politely, stay agreeable.

And so, I stayed silent. I smiled at the right moments, laughed at the right jokes, played the part. Later, laying awake replaying the evening, I realised how invisible I had made myself. How I had erased myself before anyone else even had the chance to.

That is the subtle danger of the Partner's Crown. It doesn't arrive as a command. It arrives as a whisper. Tone it down. Don't push too hard. Be softer. Be quieter. Be smaller. And because it feels like love to bend, because we convince ourselves it's devotion, we wear it without question.

But here is the truth I know now: a crown that asks you to erase yourself will never fit. Love that requires you to disappear is not love. And every time I enforced those invisible rules, I wasn't preserving connection - I was abandoning myself.

THE HEALING

Letting go of the Partner's Crown wasn't about one dramatic act. It wasn't a single day where I stood up and declared I would never shrink again. It was slower, gentler, sometimes painfully clumsy.

The first act of rebellion was small: I stopped colouring my hair blonde. To anyone else, it probably seemed like nothing, but to me it was everything. Each inch of brown was a reclamation. Each glance in the mirror became a reminder: this is me. Not the version I thought would be easier to love... but the real me.

Next, I started practising speaking up in small ways. Ordering the meal I wanted, Saying, "I don't agree," in a conversation or a text message, even if my voice trembled. Some days, I still slipped back into old patterns biting my tongue or saying sorry, smiling when I didn't feel like it. But little by little, I started hearing my own voice again. And then there was the hardest part... forgiving myself.

Because the truth is, I wasn't angry at the men or anyone else in my life. I was angry at myself. For silencing, shrinking, contorting, for years of disappearing in the name of love. It took me a long time to realise that anger wasn't punishment. It was grief. Grief for all the times I had abandoned myself.

And forgiveness, for me, meant acknowledging that I did the best I could with what I believed at the time. I wasn't foolish. I wasn't weak. I was human, longing to be loved, and I thought the path to love was paved with sacrifice.

But here's what I know now: real love does not require you to become less. Real love celebrates the fullness of who you are.

Real love makes space for your voice, your spark, your crown.

The Partner's Crown was the hardest to remove, because it was the one I placed on my own head. But learning to set it down became one of the greatest acts of love I have ever given myself.

STORIES FROM OTHER WOMEN

When I began talking about this idea of the Partner's Crown, I was surprised by how many women leaned in and said quietly, me too.

One friend told me about how she used to hide parts of herself because she thought they were "too much." She loved books, philosophy, ideas that made her feel alive - but every time she brought them up, her partner would roll his eyes. So, she stopped. For years, she played down her intelligence, until one day she realised she didn't even know what she enjoyed reading anymore. Her reclaiming began with walking into a bookstore and asking herself, "What do I want to read, just for me?"

That simple act was a spark of freedom.

Another friend admitted that she had trained herself to laugh softly. Her natural laugh was loud, unapologetic, the kind that turned heads. But she had been told it was "a bit much," so she muted it. She carried that muted laugh for years, until one night, surrounded by girlfriends, she let it out - full, wild, unrestrained. The room erupted with joy. And she realised she had been starving herself of that freedom for far too long.

And then there was a woman I met briefly, who said she stayed in a relationship because she thought her softness was her only value. She cooked the meals he liked, wore the clothes he liked, even laughed at jokes she didn't find funny. "I thought I was being loved," she told me, "But really, I was just being tolerated." Leaving wasn't the end of her story - it was the beginning. It was the moment she decided she would no longer mistake tolerance for love.

THE TRUTH ABOUT THE PARTNER'S CROWN

The Partner's Crown is never placed on our heads by one person. It is woven from the invisible rules we absorb - from society, from whispers in our culture - but the choice to wear it, to tighten it, to keep it in place, is ours.

And that's the liberating truth: if we are the ones who enforced it, then we are also the ones who can set it down.

Every time you laugh loudly without apology, you set it down.

Every time you speak the truth even when your voice shakes, you set it down. Every time you show up in your natural beauty,

your natural spark, your natural self, you set it down.

A crown that asks you to erase yourself will never fit.

The crown that was always yours is - steady, radiant, unshakable - was just waiting there for you all along.

THE CHILDREN'S CROWN

Motherhood is often spoken about as pure joy, pure love, the ultimate fulfilment. And yes, it has given me some of the deepest love I have ever known. But what is rarely talked about is the weight - the crown that slips onto your head almost unnoticed, heavy with expectation.

It is not my children who made it heavy. It was the belief that their happiness, their choices, their successes or failures, reflected my worth as their mother - and even as a woman.

When they were small, I felt as though my love alone could shield them from harm. If I worked hard enough, stayed present enough, loved fiercely enough, maybe I could guarantee their safety and happiness. But the truth is, children come into this world already themselves. They arrive with their own personalities, their own perceptions, their own paths to walk.

Over the years, raising three daughters and my son. Watching my girls step into womanhood, and seeing my son become a man. I've come to realise that so much of parenting is learning to let go.

I used to believe in the old debate of nature versus nurture, that perhaps children are entirely shaped by the way we raise them. But after mothering four unique human beings, I no longer believe it's so simple. Each of them came into this world with their own blueprint. Yes, my guidance mattered, but it did not define them. They are not extensions of me. They are their own.

And yet, for years, I carried the illusion that their lives were a mirror of mine. If they stumbled, I thought I had failed. If they hurt, I believed

I should have protected them better. If they succeeded, I allowed myself a fleeting moment of relief, as though I had earned it.

That is the weight of the Children's Crown: the belief that our worth as mothers is measured in outcomes that were never ours to control.

But beneath that illusion, there is another truth. The truth that we view our children as our heart and soul. For me it is the love that keeps me anchored, even when the rest of the world feels unsteady.

When my children read these words, I want them to know this;

You are not my achievements; you are my heart. You don't have to be perfect to be enough. You don't have to succeed to be loved. You don't have to carry my dreams. You have your own.

Motherhood has been my greatest teacher. It taught me that love cannot be measured in outcomes, and that crowns cannot be passed down like heirlooms. Each of my children has their own crown, their own worth, their own path. And mine is mine.

Letting go of the children's crown, the crown of impossible expectations - has been one of the hardest and most freeing lessons of my life.

It has allowed me to love my children not as reflections of myself, but as the whole, radiant, messy, extraordinary humans they already are.

THE SOCIETY CROWN

The heaviest crown I ever wore was not handed down or shaped inside love. It was placed on my head by the world itself... by the collective voice of society.

The Society's Crown is made entirely of "should."

It is the invisible weight of rules and expectations that tell women how to exist: what we should look like, how we should behave, what we should achieve, and how we should balance it all without complaint.

It doesn't sparkle; it suffocates.

THE RULES NO ONE HAD TO SAY OUT LOUD

Be ambitious but not intimidating.

Be beautiful, but not vain.

Be strong, but not louder than a man.

Be sexy, but not sexual.

Be a mother, but don't let it consume you.

Be youthful, but age gracefully.

Be thin, but not "too thin."

Work hard, but don't outshine others.

Speak up, but not too often.

Whatever you are, society will tell you that you are either too much of it or not enough. That is the endless paradox, and that is the weight of the Society's Crown.

How It Slipped onto My Head

I didn't notice it at first. I thought I was simply adapting, doing what was expected, being agreeable. But little by little, the weight pressed down.

It was softening my voice in a meeting because I didn't want to be called "too aggressive."

It was choosing blonde over my natural hair because I thought it made me more likeable, more palatable, more appealing.

It was smiling politely through comments that stung because I didn't want to be labelled "too sensitive."

It was holding back my laughter in case it was "too loud," or holding back my intelligence in case it made me "too intimidating."

Each of those choices seemed small, almost harmless. But together, they built a pattern. A way of existing that put everyone else's comfort above my truth.

The Society's Crown is dangerous because it convinces you that these compromises are survival - that they are the price of acceptance, the cost of belonging.

THE LIE BENEATH THE CROWN

The deepest lie the Society's Crown tells is this: if you follow the rules, you will finally be loved, safe, and enough.

But it's an illusion. The rules contradict themselves. The finish line keeps moving. No matter how hard you try, it is never enough.

I know this because I chased it. I ticked the boxes, wore the right clothes, smiled at the right jokes, made myself smaller when the room demanded it. And each time I thought I had arrived, the target shifted. It was like running toward a horizon that only stretched further away.

The cost? My voice. My confidence. My crown.

Breaking the Illusion

Loosening the Society's Crown didn't happen in a grand act of rebellion. It happened quietly, in small choices that added up.

It was walking into a room wearing what felt like me instead of what felt "appropriate." It was letting my hair return to its natural colour because it's mine, and that is enough. It was saying no to things that drained me, even if people were disappointed.

It was choosing to speak up when I had something worth saying, without softening it to make it more digestible or to make someone else feel comfortable.

The Society's Crown doesn't shatter in one moment. It is dismantled piece by piece, in acts of defiance so small they almost seem invisible. But each one is a step back to yourself.

THE TRUTH BENEATH IT ALL

The truth is this: society doesn't give us crowns; it hands us cages. The real crown, the one made of dignity, confidence, and worth... was ours all along.

Sometimes it tilts. Sometimes it feels unbearably heavy beneath the weight of judgement, comparison, and pressure. Sometimes it hides under labels and expectations. But it never disappears.

The Society's Crown loses its power the moment we stop mistaking approval for worth.

And when you lift your head, straighten your back, and wear the crown that has always been yours, you realise you were never too much, and you were never not enough.

HOW FALSE CROWNS FEEL

False crowns are easy to spot once you know the signs. They feel:

Heavy - like the responsibility of always being the dependable one, the peacemaker in the family, or the "perfect mum" who never falters.

Restrictive - the way your partner's preferences box you in, or the way your children expect you to always be available, endlessly patient, endlessly giving. Fragile - like society's demands for beauty or success, crowns that require constant upkeep and collapse the moment you slip.

Uncomfortable - they never quite fit, no matter how much you adjust yourself to wear them.

True crowns, in contrast, feel like home. They may carry responsibility, yes. But they fit your head, your heart, your soul. They don't silence you; they amplify you.

A MOMENT OF REALISATION

I remember one evening when the heaviness became undeniable. We were heading out to dinner with old friends, and I had spent nearly an hour getting ready. I chose a dress I knew he liked, smoothed my hair into the sleek style he preferred, and applied makeup that felt more like armour than decoration. By the time I was done, my reflection in the mirror was flawless but unfamiliar. She looked polished, yes. Beautiful, even. But she didn't look free.

I stood there, staring at the woman in the mirror, and felt the strangest split inside me. Outwardly, I was ready to smile, to laugh, to play the role of the woman who "had it all together." But inwardly, something inside me sagged. I realised I wasn't dressing for myself. I was dressing for approval.

And as I looked at her - at me - the thought arose uninvited: "You don't even know who you are anymore."

That thought hurt, but it also opened a door. Because in that moment, I became aware not just of him, but of all the crowns I was carrying at once: my family's hopes, his preferences, society's ideals, my children's unspoken need for me to hold everything together.

The weight of them pressed down all at once.

And then, like a clean blade cutting through the noise, another thought came: These aren't my crowns.

THE TURNING POINT

That night didn't mean I threw them all off instantly. Crowns worn for years don't tumble to the ground with one decision. Some had become welded to me through habit. Some were disguised as love, duty, or responsibility. Some were so subtle I didn't even recognise them as crowns at all.

But the recognition itself was powerful. Once you know a crown isn't yours, you can never un-know it. You may still carry it for a while, but it will never sit quite the same way again.

I began to ask myself small questions:

Does this expectation fit who I truly am?

Am I wearing this crown out of choice, or out of fear of disapproval?

If I set this crown down, what freedom might I feel?

Those questions didn't make me careless, selfish, or rebellious. They made me honest. And honesty is what lightens the load.

PRACTICAL EXERCISES: RELEASING HEAVY CROWNS

"Healing is never abstract. It needs embodiment. It needs practice."

Here are tools that helped me begin loosening the crowns that were not mine:

The Inventory of Crowns

Take a journal and write a list of all the roles and expectations you carry as a mother,

partner, daughter, colleague, friend. Then beside each, write what feels authentic and

what feels forced. This will show you where the heavy crowns sit.

The Body Check

When you agree to something, a favour, a role, a commitment. Pause and notice your body.

Does your chest tighten? Does your stomach sink? Does your throat feel constricted?

These are signs that your body is telling you. This crown is too heavy.

The Release Ritual

1. On a piece of paper, write down a crown you're ready to set down, an expectation that doesn't belong to you.
2. Burn it safely, tear it up, or bury it. Symbolic acts matter. They speak directly to the subconscious: I no longer carry this weight.

Affirmations for Lightness

Speak these daily, especially when you feel yourself bending under expectation:

- I release the crowns that do not belong to me.

- I am free to choose which crowns I wear.

- My true crown fits with ease and grace.

CHOOSING YOUR OWN CROWN

The crowns shaped by others - family, partners, children, society - often look noble. They're often offered in the language of love, duty, or pride. But if they silence your voice, smother your truth, or weigh down your spirit, they are not yours to wear.

The work of this chapter is not to cast off every crown, but to discern which ones belong to you and which ones don't. Parenthood, family ties, community roles - these may come with responsibility, but they should never demand your identity.

Your crown, the one that was yours from the beginning, is the only one that will ever truly fit. And here's the paradox: when you wear your own crown, everyone else benefits.

- Your children don't gain a mother who pretends - they gain one who is present.

- Your partner doesn't gain someone who bends to please - they gain someone authentic and alive.

- Your family, your friends, your work - they all gain the real you.

The next step is about letting go. It's about learning to see yourself clearly again not through other people's mirrors, but through your own.

"When the mirror shatters, we're left piecing together who we are from who we were."

3

SHATTERED MIRRORS

There is a particular silence that follows heartbreak. Not the quiet of peace, but the quiet of absence. After the breakup, after the weight of expectations and the heavy crowns I had carried for years, there was another layer I hadn't yet faced: the mirror.

For as long as I could remember, I had measured myself by the reflection I saw in someone else's eyes. When he looked at me with love, I felt radiant. When he praised me, I felt valuable. When he reached for my hand in public, I felt chosen, visible, proud.

But when that love left, it was as if the mirror shattered. Suddenly, there was no reflection. No confirmation. No proof that I was beautiful, worthy, or enough. I would catch sight of myself in the bathroom mirror and see only cracks, distorted fragments of the woman I thought I was.

And the thought that haunted me was simple and sharp: If he no longer sees me, do I even exist as I believed I did?

It was terrifying to realise how much of myself I had outsourced to another person's gaze. Terrifying to see how fragile my sense of worth had become the moment the mirror broke.

THE DANGER OF REFLECTED WORTH

We all begin life with mirrors. As children, our sense of self is shaped by how we are reflected to us. A smile, a nod, a word of encouragement, these are the first mirrors. They tell us: you belong, you are safe, you are loved. But somewhere along the way, mirrors become more than feedback. They become dependence. Instead of glancing at others for connection, we stare at them for definition.

We begin to believe:

I am only as beautiful as he says I am.

I am only as smart as my boss believes I am.

I am only as lovable as my parents treat me.

I am only as worthy as my friends affirm I am.

And that is where the danger lies. Because reflections are fickle. People's opinions shift. Their attention wanders. Their love may fade. And when it does, if your worth is tethered to their gaze, you crumble right alongside it.

MY OWN SHATTERED MIRROR

In the weeks after the breakup, I found myself avoiding mirrors altogether. Not just the literal ones - though I did that too - but also the metaphorical mirrors: the gaze of friends, the conversations at social events, the subtle scrutiny of people who knew my story.

I didn't want to be seen. And yet, paradoxically, I longed for it. I ached for someone, anyone, to reflect back to me what I could no longer access on my own. A look of admiration. A word of reassurance. Proof that I was still enough.

One evening, I stood in front of my bedroom mirror, half-dressed for an event I didn't even want to attend. My makeup was half-done, my hair flat, my dress tugged uncomfortably at my ribs. The reflection staring back at me looked exhausted, defeated, hollow.

I whispered to her... to me: "Who are you without his eyes on you?" "Who are you if no one sees?"

The silence that followed was deafening.

A FRIEND'S STORY

A friend once told me that after her divorce, she walked into a café alone for the first time in years. She said it felt like walking in naked. Not because anyone was staring, but because she had forgotten how to see herself outside the reflection of being "his wife."

Her story reminded me how seductive mirrors can be. They seem to offer clarity, but only as long as someone else is holding them steady. When they drop the mirror, we scramble, desperate for another one, forgetting that we've always had the power to see ourselves directly.

FUNHOUSE MIRRORS

The truth is, not all mirrors are accurate. Many are warped, like the distorted glass of a funhouse.

A partner who belittles you holds up a mirror that makes you look smaller than you are. A friend who envies you reflects a twisted version of your light. A parent who never approved shows you an image where you'll never be enough. And yet, when we are desperate, we accept even the warped reflections. We treat them as truth, forgetting that the mirror itself is flawed.

Reclaiming your crown means questioning the mirrors: Is this reflection accurate, or is it warped by their own wounds and limitations?

WHY WE CRAVE THE MIRROR

Psychologists call it "mirroring." As infants, we rely on caregivers to reflect our emotions back to us. A baby smiles, the parent smiles in return and the baby learns: I exist. I matter.

But when those early mirrors are absent, inconsistent, or distorted, we grow into adults who crave external validation like oxygen. We learn to survive by scanning faces, reading moods, moulding ourselves to fit the reflection we want to see. Heartbreak exposes this craving in its rawest form. Suddenly, the steady mirror we depended on is gone. The ache of absence feels unbearable. But here's the truth: the ache isn't weakness. It's wiring. Healing begins when we build an internal mirror, one that reflects truth regardless of who is watching.

The ache isn't weakness. It's wiring. Healing begins when we build an internal mirror, one that reflects truth regardless of who is watching.

THE PRACTICE OF SELF-RECOGNITION

Learning to see yourself without relying on others is not instant. It takes practice. But it is the most powerful work you will ever do. Here are some practices that helped me:

Mirror Work

Stand in front of a mirror. Look into your own eyes. Say: I see you. I honour you. I love you. The first time, you might cry. The second, you might cringe. The third, you may begin to believe.

The No-Mirror Day

Spend one day without checking mirrors. Get dressed, smile, eat, move - without assessing how it looks. Notice how freeing it is to live from the inside out.

Journalling

Write: Who am I without anyone else's gaze? Who am I when no one is watching? Keep writing until the answers arrive.

Compliment Reversal

When someone gives you a compliment, repeat it back to yourself later. Anchor it inside. Let it become yours, not just theirs.

Window Work

Catch your reflection unexpectedly - in shop windows, in the dark screen of your phone and instead of criticising, simply nod at yourself. Acknowledge: There you are.

A STORY OF REBUILDING

There came a day when I walked into a room alone - no partner's hand to hold, no friend by my side. The familiar panic rose: Who will reflect me now?

Then, in a window across the room, I caught my own reflection. For once, I didn't flinch. I lifted my head, steadied my breath, and thought I am enough, even if no one is watching.

It wasn't arrogance. It was truth. For the first time, I was my own mirror.

SEEING YOURSELF CLEARLY

Mirrors can shatter. Reflections can fade. But your crown remains. This part isn't about rejecting love or affirmation. It's about reclaiming the power to see yourself clearly, even in their absence.

When you stop living only through the reflections of others, you begin to live in the light of your own crown. And that is where true freedom begins.

The next step is learning how to gather the fragments of yourself and begin again. Because once the mirror shatters, you can't piece it back exactly as it was. But you can create something new -something stronger, clearer, and truer to who you are.

"And one day when you look back,

you will see what you could not then.

The crown you are building now

shines brighter than before."

"Not because its perfect,

but because it carries the light of your resilience."

4

PICKING UP THE PIECES

ROCK BOTTOM

We live in a world that loves neat stories. The before-and-after photos. The glow-ups. The Instagram captions about hitting rock bottom one month and building an empire the next. We are sold the idea that healing should look like a staircase you climb, step by step, never slipping back.

But healing doesn't look like that.

Healing is not linear. It is not glamorous. It doesn't come with triumphant music swelling in the background or a crowd cheering you on. Healing does not arrive on schedule, and it certainly doesn't fit into a caption or a photo.

Healing looks like this:

Three days of progress where you feel strong, only to collapse in tears on the fourth.

A week of calm that suddenly gives way to a wave of grief so strong you double over in your car.

Smiling at breakfast, then crying silently in the supermarket aisle because a song plays over the speakers that reminds you of him.

A morning walk where you breathe easily, followed by an afternoon where getting dressed feels impossible.

At first, I thought these stumbles meant I was failing. I thought healing was meant to be about getting better every day, about never slipping backwards, about holding steady once you found your footing. Each collapse felt like proof that I was broken beyond repair.

But slowly, I came to see it differently. Healing is not about erasing the pain. It is about learning to walk alongside it. The backward steps, the spirals, the stumbles - they are not failures. They are evidence of being human. They are evidence that you are still moving, still trying, still alive.

THE MOSAIC METAPHOR

One afternoon, I wandered into a gallery and stopped in front of a mosaic. From across the room, it glittered, beautiful and whole. But up close, I saw the truth: it was made entirely from fragments. Jagged pieces of broken glass. Shards of tile. Chips of pottery that someone else might have thrown away.

Each piece, on its own, looked useless. But together, they formed something breathtakingly beautiful.

And it struck me: this is what healing is.

We are mosaics. The pieces of ourselves that feel broken are not wasted. They are not evidence of failure. When gathered carefully, they create something entirely new - not what we were before, but something richer, more layered, more resilient.

Your crown may feel shattered, but every fragment has a place. Every time you breathe through pain, every time you choose to get up, every time you show yourself compassion - you are laying another piece into the mosaic of your crown.

MY FIRST PIECES

After the lighthouse, the very first piece I picked up was journalling. It wasn't polished or profound. Some mornings, I only managed a few words: angry, tired, lonely. Other days, I scrawled long sentences across the page: Today I survived. Sometimes the ink blurred where my tears had fallen. It didn't matter. The act of writing was the act of remembering myself. Each word was a fragment reclaimed.

The second piece was breathwork. I began with three minutes a day. I would set a timer, close my eyes, and focus only on breathing: in for four, hold for four, out for four. Some days, I sobbed through it. Some days, I fell asleep. Some days, I felt nothing at all. But each time, I stayed. Each time, I proved to myself: I can sit with this. I can carry this.

The third piece was walking. At first, just to the letterbox. Then around the block. Then, eventually, to the beach. Each step felt heavy at first, like dragging myself through mud. But then something subtle happened: my body reminded me that I was still alive. My legs carried me. My lungs filled with air. The sea spread wide before me. Even when I felt broken, my body whispered: you are still here.

These pieces, on their own, didn't look like much. But stacked together, they became a foundation. And over time, I began to see: healing doesn't happen in leaps. It happens in fragments.

A FRIEND'S PIECES

I wasn't alone in this. A friend who had lost her partner once told me that her first piece was painting. She had never painted before - she wasn't an artist. But she bought cheap brushes and tubs of paint and began covering canvas after canvas in colour. Swirls. Lines. Mess. "It wasn't about making something beautiful," she told me. "It was about giving my grief somewhere to live."

Another friend said her first piece was cooking. She had spent years making only the meals her husband liked. When he left, she realised she didn't even know what she liked. So, she experimented. Burnt meals. Strange flavour combinations. Joyful discoveries. "Cooking became my way of saying: I'm still here. I still matter."

Another friend told me his first piece was music. He would put on the songs he used to love as a teenager, turn the volume up high, and let himself sing until his throat ached. "It reminded me of who I was before anyone told me who to be," he said.

Their pieces were different. But the point wasn't what the pieces were. The point was that they were theirs.

WHY SMALL WINS MATTER

When your crown feels shattered, the idea of grand transformation is overwhelming. You don't need to climb a mountain. You don't need to reinvent your life overnight. What you need is the smallest possible act of remembering.

Getting out of bed is a win. Brushing your teeth is a win.

Taking a shower, even if you cry through it, is a win. Drinking a glass of water is a win.

Saying "no" when your whole life has been built on saying "yes" is a win.

These small wins matter because they stack. Quietly. Patiently. They rebuild your sense of self, one moment at a time.

PRACTICES FOR PICKING UP PIECES

The Three Wins Journal

Each night, write down three wins from the day. No win is too small. If all you did was breathe through a panic attack, that counts. If all you did was put on clean socks, that counts.

Breathwork for Fragmented Days

Set a timer for three minutes. Close your eyes. Inhale slowly, count to four. Hold for four. Exhale for four. Hold for four. Repeat. As you breathe, imagine your scattered pieces returning home to you.

The Ritual of Choice

Each day, make one deliberate choice for yourself. It could be as small as choosing the mug you love, or as big as saying no to something that drains you. Each choice says: I still have agency.

Reclaiming Joys

Make a list of small joys that belong only to you. Reading in the sun. Dancing barefoot in the kitchen. Drinking tea from your favourite cup. Commit to one joy every single day.

ASK YOURSELF

What small wins have you already experienced, even if you dismissed them? What pieces of yourself feel broken — and how might they fit into your mosaic? What choice can you make today that belongs entirely to you?

What joy can you reclaim this week, no matter how small?

THE CROWN AS A MOSAIC

Healing is not about gluing your old life back together as though nothing ever happened. That life is gone. Healing is about creating something new with the pieces you still hold. Your crown may have felt shattered, but every act of care, every small decision, every fragile step forward is another jewel placed back into it.

There will be days when it doesn't feel like progress, it will feel like survival. When your hands shake as you lift another shard and wonder if it's worth the weight. But keep going because this isn't about rebuilding the life you had. It's about becoming the person you were always ment to be.

You're not starting from scratch, although at times you will feel like you are. You are starting from experience. And that is a different kind of strength.

It's built. It's real. It's yours.

And one day, when you look back, you will see something you couldn't at the time: the crown you are building now shines brighter than before.

Not because it is perfect, but because it carries the light of your resilience.

"Forgiveness has a quiet kind of power.
It wasn't for him; it was for me.

It was the moment I decided to stop bleeding
for what cut too deep, for too long.

And in that moment,
I stepped back into my own light,
lifted my head, and walked forward.

strong and completely unbound."

5

THE CROWN OF FREEDOM

I remember one morning, sitting on my balcony with a cup of coffee that had long since turned cold. The steam had faded, the taste was bitter, and still, I held it, staring into the bottom of the cup as if the answer might somehow appear.

The air was still, almost heavy, and my mind was anything but. It looped the same stories on repeat: the words I had said, the ones I wished I hadn't, the silence I couldn't fill. I replayed everything, searching for meaning in the mess, believing that if I just went over, it one more time, I might uncover a hidden code - The exact reason it all fell apart.

His final words felt sharper each time I thought about them, and somehow, even the silence he left behind began to make sense. I started wishing I'd done everything differently. I thought that if I replayed it enough, I might uncover some unknown truth. Something that would finally make it all make sense.

But no matter how many times I replayed it, I was never going to find the answer. Because it wasn't mine to find.

And as the truth settled in, something inside loosened.

What he thought of me, what he said, what he did, It wasn't my business. That was his story, his mirror, his work. Mine was to stop twisting myself into shapes to understand it.

When you let what isn't yours turn you inside out, you're not punishing them, you are only punishing yourself. It's like pouring acid into your own hands and wondering why you burn.

That morning on the balcony, with the bitter taste of cold coffee in my mouth, I realised something: the only way forward wasn't in rehashing, or tallying, or clinging to pain. The only way forward was forgiveness, not for him, but for me.

PAIN IS ADDICTIVE

We don't like to admit it, but pain can be intoxicating. It gives us something to hold onto when everything else has slipped through our fingers. It becomes a familiar companion. Bitter, yes, but reliable.

For a long time, I didn't realise I was addicted to my own pain. It wasn't loud or obvious. It was that soft, insidious whisper that creeps into your thoughts when you least expect it, quietly reminding you of the proof, replaying the scenes, recounting the betrayals.

It whispers, "See?" "You deserve to hurt."

It deceives you when you are most vulnerable, because pain enjoys company. It feeds on your fear, your confusion, your longing. It convinces you that if you keep replaying the story, eventually you'll find peace. But that's the cruel trick of it, this kind of pain has no interest in peace.

And so, you feed it. Over and over.

You pick the wound open again and again, telling yourself you're trying to understand. You tally up the wrongs, rehearse the arguments, rewrite the ending,

all in the name of closure.

But closure doesn't come that way.

Pain is seductive because it offers the illusion of control. When everything else has fallen apart, pain gives you something to do. It allows you sit in the ruins and feel productive, as though analysing the ache will somehow rewrite the story.

I would go over the ways I'd been wronged - Tally his betrayals, his careless words, his absence. I'd replay arguments in my head, crafting sharp comebacks I never got to say. And though I told myself I hated it, I kept doing it.

Because pain, in it's own twisted way, made me feel connected. Connected to him. Connected to what was lost. Connected to the proof that it had all meant something.

But here's what I realised later: Pain isn't only a wound. It's a form of confusion. It's the unprocessed meaning we attach to the hurt.

We don't break because of what happened.

We break because of what we made it mean about ourselves.

That is the quiet truth beneath every ache.

"They left me." - I must be unlovable

"It failed." - I must be a failure

"They didn't see me." - I must be invisible

"They moved on." - I must be replaceable

That's the scar that stays. That's what keeps us picking at the wound. But healing begins the moment you whisper a new truth back to yourself:

"It wasn't your fault. But it became your belief that it was."

And that belief is what we need to unlearn. Because when you stop feeding pain and start reframing the meaning, you begin to reclaim you crown.

Piece by piece, thought by thought.

FORGIVENESS IS FOR YOU

That's when I learned something I had resisted for years: forgiveness is not for them. It's for you.

Forgiveness doesn't mean condoning what they did. It doesn't mean excusing it or pretending it didn't cut deep. It doesn't mean you let them back into your life. Forgiveness simply means you stop drinking the poison. You stop letting the story run you ragged. You stop letting the mirror of someone else's choices dictate how you see yourself.

When you forgive, you set yourself free.

And let me tell you - I fought this truth. I told myself forgiveness meant weakness, surrender, letting him "win." But one day, I understood: forgiveness was strength.

Forgiveness was not letting him live rent-free in my head any longer. Forgiveness was a crown I could finally wear without it slipping.

THE UNIVERSE HAS ITS LESSONS

The universe has a funny way of teaching us. At the time, it often feels cruel, as though life is working against us, denying us the things we desperately want. But looking back, I see it differently.

The universe is never against us. It is always for us.

When something or someone is taken away, it can feel like rejection. Our ego is bruised. We feel abandoned, unseen, unwanted. But in reality, rejection is redirection. It is life saying: not this, not here, not with them.

At the time, I thought I had lost everything. In truth, I had lost only the illusion. What wasn't meant for me was being cleared away. What remained was space - space for the real, the aligned, the true.

Forgiveness allowed me to pause and see that. To stop fighting reality and start trusting that even the hardest lessons were leading me somewhere.

THE CROWN AND FORGIVENESS

When I forgave, I didn't forget. I didn't erase the lessons, the boundaries, the truths I had uncovered. But I laid down the weight. I stopped carrying his choices as though they defined me.

Forgiveness became the act of lifting my crown back onto my head. Not because he placed it there, but because I remembered it was mine.

And here's the thing: forgiveness is not a one-time act. It's a practice. Some days you forgive once. Other days, you forgive fifty times before lunch. But each time you do, the crown steadies. Each time you do, you remind yourself: my worth is not tethered to anyone else's actions.

PRACTICES FOR FORGIVENESS

The Tally Release

If you find yourself keeping score, write the list down - every wrong, every hurt. Then, when you're ready, burn it, tear it, release it. Let the ashes remind you: this does not belong to me anymore.

The Balcony Pause

Sit with a cup of coffee or tea. Imagine all the opinions, distortions, and hurts you've been carrying.

Whisper to yourself:

"What they think or say is none of my business. My peace is my business."

Mirror Work for Forgiveness

Stand before the mirror and say:

"I forgive not for them, but for me. I forgive because I deserve peace. I forgive because I am free."

The Universe Trust Practice

Each time rejection stings, pause and whisper:

> "The universe is for me, not against me. If this has left, it was not mine to hold."

THE FREEDOM OF FORGIVENESS

Forgiveness is not about them. It is not about rewriting the past. It is about reclaiming your crown, steady and untouchable. The universe, in its infinite wisdom, clears away what doesn't belong, even when we cling to it. Forgiveness is how we unclench our fists. It's how we make space for what is truly meant for us.

And here's the most radical truth I discovered: forgiveness is proof of love. Not just for them, but for myself. Because I loved myself enough to stop hurting. I loved myself enough to choose peace. Forgiveness is the crown polished, radiant, lifted high.

"The crown within never slips.

It is the quiet knowing that lives beneath the noise,

the compass that whispers when the world demands you shout.

When you learn to listen to it, you realise you were never lost,

only waiting to come home to yourself."

6

THE CROWN WITHIN

A QUIET MOMENT

It happened on a morning when nothing seemed special. I was sitting on my balcony waiting for the sun to rise with a cup of coffee, staring at the steam rising into the air. All was quiet, unusually still. There were no demands, no conversations, no distractions. Just me and the silence.

At first, the quiet felt uncomfortable. My thoughts rushed in, restless and noisy. What if I never feel whole again? What if I never love again? What if this is it?

But then, beneath the noise, I felt something softer. A pulse. A whisper. It wasn't dramatic. It wasn't even words. It was simply a knowing, deep in my chest: You are here. You are whole. Keep going.

It was the first time I realised the crown wasn't only something I wore on the outside. It lived within me, steady, guiding me like a compass. Even when my outer crown had slipped, even when heartbreak and expectations had weighed me down, the inner crown had never stopped glowing.

THE OUTER CROWN VS. THE INNER CROWN

The outer crown is what others can see. It's in the way you carry yourself, the confidence in your step, the sparkle in your eye. It's what people comment on - your success, your style, your strength. But the outer crown is only a reflection. It is fragile because it can tilt, slip, or grow heavy when you forget yourself.

The inner crown, though - that cannot be touched. It is not for display. It is not for approval. It is your soul's compass, the part of you that knows your truth even when the world shouts otherwise. When you reconnect with your inner crown, the outer one naturally steadies. You no longer rely on mirrors or expectations to keep it in place. You walk with quiet certainty, not because you're trying to prove anything, but because you are anchored in who you are.

LISTENING TO THE SOUL COMPASS

The inner crown speaks quietly. It doesn't shout. It doesn't demand. It whispers.

You feel it in the unease that rises when you're about to say yes to something you don't want. You feel it in the relief that washes over you when you finally speak the truth. You feel it in the goosebumps that appear when a decision aligns with your deepest self. For years, I ignored this compass. I silenced it with busyness, drowned it out with other people's opinions, second-guessed it until I couldn't hear it anymore. But when I began to pick up the pieces of my life, I realised I couldn't rebuild without it. I needed the compass. I needed the crown within.

A STORY OF TRUSTING THE COMPASS

I remember being invited to a social event not long after the breakup. My first instinct was to say yes - to prove I was fine, to show up polished and smiling, to let others reflect an image of resilience I didn't actually feel.

But something in me whispered: Not yet. Rest. I ignored it at first. I told myself I was being lazy, antisocial, weak. But the whisper returned, steady: Rest. Stay home.

So, for the first time, I listened. I stayed in. I cooked myself a simple meal, wrote in my journal, and watched the moon rise from my balcony. It wasn't glamorous. But it was honest.

And afterwards, I felt a peace I hadn't felt in months. That was my inner crown guiding me. That was my compass saying: Choose what is true, not what looks good.

A FRIEND'S STORY

A friend of mine had built her life around a career that looked perfect from the outside. She had the title, the salary, the respect.

Her outer crown glittered. But inside, she was exhausted, burnt out, and miserable.

One day, she said she sat in her car in the office carpark and burst into tears. The thought of walking into the building made her stomach twist. That twist was her inner crown speaking. For years, she had ignored it, telling herself she "should" be grateful. But that day, she finally listened. Within months, she had left her job and begun building a business aligned with her passions.

She told me later: "It wasn't easy, but it was real. For the first time, I was following my compass instead of everyone else's map."

THE COURAGE TO LISTEN

Listening to your inner crown takes courage. It often asks you to choose rest when the world demands hustle. To say no when others expect yes. To step away when staying would be easier. It can feel terrifying - because the outer crown loves approval, and the inner crown often requires risking it. But here's the paradox: the more you honour the inner crown, the steadier the outer crown becomes. When your choices align with your soul, you radiate a confidence that no external approval can match.

PRACTICES FOR CONNECTING TO THE CROWN WITHIN

THE STILLNESS RITUAL

Set aside five minutes each day for stillness. No phone, no music, no conversation. Sit. Breathe. Ask: What does my crown within want me to know today?

Compass Journalling

At the top of a page, write:

What feels true for me right now?

Let your hand move without censoring.

Don't edit.

Trust what comes.

The Body as Compass

Your body often feels truth before your mind does.

Pay attention:

does your chest expand (yes) or contract (no)?

> Does your stomach relax (alignment) or knot (misalignment)?
>
> **Crown Check for Decisions**
>
> Before saying yes or no, pause.
>
> Ask: Does this choice honour my crown, or does it weigh it down?

ASK YOURSELF

When was the last time you felt your inner compass speaking? Did you listen? What does your crown within feel like - a whisper, a sensation, a knowing? Where in your life are you ignoring the compass because it risks disapproval?

THE LIGHT WITHIN

The outer crown can slip, but the inner crown never leaves. It is your compass, your anchor, your steady flame.

When you learn to listen to it, you realise that worth was never about appearances, approval, or performance. Worth was always about alignment - about living from the quiet, radiant truth within.

This is where true confidence is born. Not from proving, not from pleasing, but from living in harmony with your soul.

And once you are anchored in your crown within, you are ready for the next step: to release your grip on what isn't yours, to practise the art of letting go.

That is the power of detachment - the freedom waiting in Chapter 7.

"Detachment isn't letting go of love, it's letting go of the illusion that love can be controlled."

7

THE POWER OF DETACHMENT

WHEN CLINGING BECOMES A CAGE

There was a season in my life when I clung so tightly to what was leaving that I barely had energy for anything else. I replayed conversations endlessly, analysing every word. I scrolled through social media, searching for clues. I checked my phone constantly, desperate for a message that never came.

I told myself it was love, but it wasn't. It was fear. Fear of rejection. Fear of being unseen. Fear that without him, I had no worth. Because he made me feel strong, and without his strength, I thought I would lose mine. The tighter I clung, the smaller I became. I was gripping the edges of a cage I didn't realise I was trapped in, a cage that I'd trapped myself in, locked and threw away the key. But a cage none the less. And then, one afternoon, exhausted and numb, I whispered to myself: I don't care anymore. It wasn't bitterness. It wasn't anger. In the end, all that was left was to surrender.

The moment I said those words, I felt lighter. My body softened. My breath deepened. I realised that letting go wasn't about losing. It was about remembering that my crown was never theirs to hold in the first place.

That was the beginning of detachment.

WHAT DETACHMENT IS (AND ISN'T)

Detachment is one of the most misunderstood powers. Many people hear the word and think it means apathy, coldness, emotional walls. But true detachment is none of these things.

Detachment is not:
- Shutting down your heart.
- Pretending you don't care when you actually do.
- Withdrawing from love, connection, or joy.

Detachment is:
- Refusing to let your worth rise and fall with someone else's choices.
- Releasing the grip on outcomes you cannot control.
- Standing in your strength, certain in yourself, regardless of who stays or leaves.

- It is the difference between gripping life with clenched fists and holding it with open hands.

THE METAPHOR OF THE OPEN HAND

I once heard someone say: "Love with an open hand, not a closed fist." When you grip too tightly, you crush what you're trying to hold. You suffocate it, strangle it, strip it of air. But when you hold with an open hand, what is meant to stay will stay. What is meant to leave will leave. And either way, you remain whole.

Detachment is the open hand. It's trusting that your crown does not depend on what you hold.

A PERSONAL STORY OF DETACHMENT

I remember a day when I was co-parenting with my ex and a situation spiralled out of my control. The old me would have obsessed, texted endlessly, argued, clung to being "right." But this time, something inside me shifted.

I repeated quietly: I don't care. Everyone's obsessed with me. Everyone loves me.

The words made me laugh at first. They felt absurd, playful. But as I repeated them, something loosened in me. I stopped caring about winning the argument. I stopped needing him to see my side. I cared only about my peace.

And in that space, I felt free. I wasn't shackled to his opinion. My crown remained steady.

A FRIEND'S STORY

A friend of mine once told me she had been in a relationship where she constantly over-gave. She said yes to everything, compromised on everything, moulded herself until she barely recognised who she was.

When it ended, she was devastated. But she also felt strangely relieved.

She said, "I realised I had been trying to hold water in my hands. No matter how tight I gripped, it kept slipping through. Letting go didn't mean I stopped loving. It meant I stopped drowning."

Her story is detachment in action. Not coldness.

Freedom.

THE MANTRA OF DETACHMENT

I began to practise a mantra that changed everything:

"I don't care. Everyone's obsessed with me.
Everyone loves me."

On the surface, it sounds arrogant, even ridiculous. But here's the secret: it isn't about arrogance. It's about loosening the grip of fear.

When I said, "I don't care," I wasn't dismissing my heart. I was dismissing the obsession with outcomes that I couldn't control.

When I said, "Everyone's obsessed with me," I wasn't claiming literal obsession. I was reminding myself that I am magnetic, radiant, enough.

When I said, "Everyone loves me," I wasn't denying conflict. I was choosing to live in the energy of being loved, not rejected. The mantra was a crown-straightener. Each time I said it, I felt taller, lighter, freer.

WHY DETACHMENT FEELS LIKE POWER

Clinging feels desperate, unworthy, and not good enough. Detachment feels light, free, whole. When you are detached, you stop chasing. You stop begging. You stop bending yourself into shapes to earn what is already yours. You become magnetic. People sense your freedom, your ease, your lightness. You radiate a quiet luxury, tthe luxury of not needing to grip life to feel worthy.

That is the power of detachment: you lift your crown with grace, and the world adjusts around you.

PRACTICES FOR DETACHMENT

The Mantra Ritual

Each morning, stand in front of the mirror, lift your head, and say:

"I don't care. Everyone's obsessed with me. Everyone loves me."

Repeat until you smile.

The smile is proof the crown is settling.

Cord-Cutting Visualisation

Close your eyes.

Picture the person, outcome, or expectation you are clinging to.

Imagine a golden cord connecting you. With love, thank them for what they taught you.

Then gently cut the cord and watch your crown glow brighter.

The Detachment Journal

Write down everything you're gripping too tightly. Then for each one, write:

This does not define my crown. I release it.

The Open-Hand Practice

Physically open your hands and whisper:

"What is mine will stay. What is not will go. Either way, I remain whole."

Ask Yourself

Where are you gripping life with a closed fist? What would it look like to hold this with an open hand? What outcomes, people, or opinions are you ready to release? How does your crown feel when you let go?

THE TRUTH BENEATH IT ALL

Detachment is not rejection. It is not indifference. It is the art of letting go. When you detach from outcomes and opinions, you remember that your worth is not negotiable. You remember that the crown was always yours. You breathe easier. You laugh more. You walk taller. This is the quiet power of detachment: the freedom to live from truth, not from fear.

When you finally detach, you begin to see things for what they really are.

Not through emotion, not through fear, and not through the noise of needing to be understood, but through truth. Detachment clears the fog. And when the fog clears, honesty becomes possible.

You start to realise that being honest with your words isn't just about how you speak to others. More importantly, it's about how you speak to yourself. Because the words you whisper when no one is listening are the ones that shape your reality. Every sentence becomes a choice; to stay stuck in the story, or to tell a new one. And then you begin to show yourself kindness, you stop bleeding for what was never yours to carry. Once you detach, your mind will stop making assumptions, and you will stop building pain from illusions.

Detachment doesn't make you cold.

It makes you clear.

It allows you to respond, not react.

To express, not explain.

To live from truth, not from fear.

Once you reach that point, you can finally be honest with yourself, with others, with life. You no longer twist your words to protect your ego or avoid discomfort. You no longer say "yes" when your soul means "no." You stop apologising for who you are. Because when you detach from outcomes, honesty becomes easy. And peace follows.

My dad always told me, "Do your best." For years I thought that meant effort, pushing, proving, performing. But now I see that it means something much deeper. Doing your best means showing up for yourself in truth, no more, no less. It means speaking from your heart without trying to be perfect. It means letting go of the stories, the assumptions, the fear, and simply doing what you can from a place of love. When you do that, there's no room left for self-judgement. Only compassion. Only peace.

That's the gift of detachment, it brings you back to your truth.

And once you live there, your words, your choices, and your energy begin to align.

That's when everything starts to change.

" Quiet luxury is walking into any room knowing you don't need to perform, because your peace speaks louder than presence."

8

QUIET LUXURY OF THE SOUL

A DIFFERENT KIND OF RADIANCE

There was an evening when I was invited to a gathering I didn't want to attend. For weeks, I had been avoiding social events, afraid of what people might think, afraid of being pitied, afraid of being seen as broken.

But something in me shifted that night. I didn't want to perform, but I also didn't want to hide.

So, I chose differently.

I wore something simple - not the most glamorous dress, not the boldest colour, just something that felt like me. I didn't do my hair perfectly. I didn't pile on makeup.

I took a deep breath before walking in and whispered: The crown is mine. I don't need to prove it.

When I entered the room, I didn't try to be the loudest or the brightest. I just was.

And to my surprise, people noticed. Not because I was putting on a show, but because I wasn't. They leaned in closer when I spoke. They smiled warmly. Someone even said, "You look so calm. So grounded."

That was the first time I understood the meaning of quiet luxury.

WHAT QUIET LUXURY REALLY MEANS

In our culture, the word "luxury" often means wealth. Designer labels, expensive handbags, extravagant holidays. But quiet luxury has nothing to do with possessions.

Quiet luxury is a state of being. It is the elegance of knowing your worth without needing to announce it. It is the crown you wear not with noise, but with grace.

It's in the way you carry yourself, the way you choose with intention, the way you live aligned with your values.

Quiet luxury says: I don't need to prove myself. I simply am.

THE CROWN AS QUIET LUXURY

Your crown is the ultimate quiet luxury. It isn't showy. It isn't desperate. It doesn't scream for attention. *It glows. It radiates.* It communicates without words:

I know who I am. I know what I carry. I know my worth.

When you wear your crown like this, you stop chasing validation. You stop performing. You begin to live in a way that is *calm, steady, magnetic.*

This is luxury. Not because it's expensive, but because it's rare.

A PERSONAL STORY

I remember the first time I walked into a café alone after heartbreak. For months, the thought had terrified me. I imagined people staring, whispering: She's alone. She's been left. She's not enough.

But one day, I decided to go. I dressed in something comfortable. I ordered my favourite coffee. I sat by the window and opened a book.

At first, I felt exposed. But as the minutes passed, I noticed something unexpected. No one was judging. In fact, no one seemed to care. And those who did glance my way looked more curious than critical. For the first time, I felt what it was to carry myself with quiet luxury - not because I was dressed in labels, not because I had someone across the table, but because I sat with my crown steady, my head high, and my heart calm.

A FRIEND'S STORY

A friend once told me that after leaving a toxic relationship, she began rebuilding her wardrobe. Not with expensive brands, but with clothes that made her feel at home in her skin.

She said, "I stopped thinking, *'Would he like this?'* and started thinking, *'Do I like this?'*

She described standing in front of the mirror one morning in a simple white shirt and jeans, nothing extraordinary. But she said she felt radiant - more radiant than she ever had in a glittering dress chosen for someone else's gaze.

That is quiet luxury. The glow of alignment.

PRACTICES FOR QUIET LUXURY

The Intentional Choice

Each morning, make one choice that feels aligned with you - a fragrance, an outfit, a meal, a word. Ask: Does this honour my crown?

The Posture of Presence

When you walk into a room, pause. Breathe. Lift your head. Imagine your crown steady. Enter slowly, intentionally. Watch how the room shifts when you don't rush to perform.

The Simplification Ritual

Declutter one small area of your life - your desk, your wardrobe, your calendar. Remove what doesn't align with your values. Quiet luxury thrives in simplicity.

The Crown Mantra

Whisper to yourself before any gathering: I don't need to prove my crown. I simply wear it.

ASK YOURSELF

What moments in your life have felt like quiet luxury, even without material wealth?

Where are you still trying to prove your worth, rather than embodying it?

What small daily choices could bring you back into alignment with your crown?

THE SOUL'S QUIET GLOW

Quiet luxury is not about what you own. It's about how you carry yourself. It is the freedom of no longer performing. The ease of living aligned with your values. The calm of knowing your worth is steady, regardless of circumstance. This is how your crown shines, not in glittering display, but in quiet radiance.

And once you begin to live from this place, you are ready for the next step: rebuilding the self you thought you lost. Because the truth is, she was never gone - she was waiting for you to choose her again.

*"Rebuilding yourself isn't about becoming someone new,
it's about returning to the woman you were
before the world told you who to be.
Piece by piece, choice by choice, you remember her.
And that remembrance is where your power begins."*

9

REBUILDING SELF

THE STRANGER IN THE MIRROR

One morning I opened my wardrobe and it felt as though I was staring into a stranger's life. The rows of dresses hanging neatly in place weren't mine. They were costumes I had worn to keep love, to keep peace, to keep the illusion of being chosen. dresses bought for events I no longer attended; nights I no longer belonged to. Shoes with heels that pinched my feet, purchased not because I loved them, but because I knew he would glance down at them and nod his approval. Blouses in colours that drained me - pale pinks and icy blues that never felt like me - but had pleased him once, so I wore them again and again until they became a uniform.

Barefoot on the carpet, hair limp around my shoulders, I stood frozen. The morning light spilled across the wardrobe doors and caught on the fabrics, and for a moment it was as though I was staring at a museum exhibit: "The Life of a Woman Who Forgot Herself."

I whispered into the silence, almost afraid to hear my own voice:

Who even am I without him?

The question landed heavily in my chest, reverberating through me as though it had been waiting to be asked. My throat tightened. My body sagged. It wasn't just about the clothes. It wasn't even about him, not really. It was about the hollow ache of not recognising the woman in the mirror anymore.

Somewhere along the way, I had blurred the line between myself and the version of me I had carefully curated to be loved. The version who wore the right colours, the right dresses, the right smile. The version who muted her voice when it felt too loud. The version who bent and shaped herself into what she thought was lovable.

And when he left, it felt as though that version left too - leaving me with nothing but the raw, unrecognisable woman beneath.

For weeks afterwards, the question haunted me: Who am I now? It followed me into the shower, into my car, into the quiet moments before bed. I searched for myself in the reflection of the bathroom mirror, in the faces of my children, in conversations with friends. But everywhere I looked, I saw gaps. I saw absence.

It was like walking into a house after the furniture had been taken out - the shape of things still visible, but the substance gone. The life I had built around him had collapsed, and I didn't know where mine began.

But here's what I didn't see at first: absence creates space. Space for questions. Space for breath. Space for rebuilding.

And slowly - so slowly it was almost imperceptible - piece by piece, I began to rebuild. Not with the old costumes or borrowed colours, but with fragments of truth. With choices that felt like me. With the faint, fragile memory that I had once existed before all of this - and that she, that woman, was still here.

THE ILLUSION OF DISAPPEARANCE

Heartbreak convinces you that you've lost yourself completely. You tell yourself you've become invisible. You look at old photos and don't recognise the smile. You hear your own laugh, and it sounds foreign. You carry yourself like a stranger in your own skin.

But the truth is: you never disappear. The essence of you is never lost. It may get buried under compromise, silenced under expectation, painted over by someone else's preferences. But it remains - waiting for you to strip away the layers and return.

Rebuilding isn't about "finding" someone new. It's about remembering the woman who was always there and choosing her again.

THE BRUSHSTROKES OF IDENTITY

Identity isn't something you stumble upon once and then keep neatly folded in a drawer for the rest of your life. It is not a single revelation, nor a fixed state of being. Identity is a living canvas - always shifting, always receiving new colours, new shapes, new textures. It is not painted in a single stroke of genius, but in the slow layering of countless moments. The way you choose what to wear in the morning. The way you move your body when you walk into a room - head lowered or lifted high. The rituals you create, like the morning cup of coffee as you watch the sun rise, or the nightly journal that helps you sift through the chaos in your brain. The passions you nurture, whether it's reading, painting, running, writing, or simply taking time to watch the clouds. Every choice, no matter how small, is a brushstroke on this canvas. Even the choices you dismiss as insignificant - the music you listen to, the way you decorate your space, the boundaries you set - they all leave their mark.

At first, standing before the canvas of your identity can feel overwhelming. Blank space is intimidating. You may ask yourself, where do I even begin? What colours belong to me? What strokes are truly mine and which ones have I borrowed from someone else?

In the beginning, it feels safer to copy what others are painting. To mimic the palettes of your family, your friends, your partner, society. You pick up the colours they hand you, even when they don't quite fit, and you convince yourself they must be right because everyone else is using them too. And so, your canvas fills - but it doesn't feel like yours. That's why, when heartbreak or loss or any great unraveling comes, it feels like the canvas has been wiped bare. The images you once recognised are suddenly gone, erased by the ending of a chapter you thought defined you. You look at the canvas and panic: *Who am I without them? Who am I without this life I built?*

But here is the truth: the canvas was never gone. It was always there, waiting. What disappears are the borrowed strokes, the colours that never belonged to you in the first place. What remains is the raw surface, ready to be painted again - this time with hues that belong to you. And so you begin, tentatively. A single stroke at first - perhaps choosing clothes that feel like you rather than ones that fit someone else's preferences. Another stroke - speaking up when your instinct is to stay silent. Another still - making time for something that nourishes you, even if no one else understands why it matters.

The canvas slowly begins to take shape. Not in a dramatic masterpiece overnight, but in the quiet consistency of showing up for yourself each day. Some strokes are bold, declaring loudly: This is me. Others are faint, almost hesitant, whispers across the canvas. Some may even be painted over later as you realise, they no longer fit. That's the beauty of a living canvas: it is never finished, and it never needs to be.

Identity is not about finding one perfect image and clinging to it. It is about allowing yourself to evolve. To add depth, to shift shades, to blend the past with the present. It is about realising that even the mistakes - the messy, uneven brushstrokes - have a place. They add texture. They make the canvas richer. And one day, you step back, and instead of seeing fragments or borrowed images, you see a picture that feels undeniably, unquestionably yours. It may not be perfect. It may not be symmetrical. But it is alive. It is true.

Your identity, your crown, is not static. It is a living artwork - one that only you can create.

MY OWN REBUILDING

I started with my wardrobe. It sounds simple, even superficial, but it wasn't. Piece by piece, I pulled clothes from the hangers, each one carrying a story. The dresses I had worn because he admired them - clinging, glittering, chosen to please. The shoes bought for dinners and events I no longer attended, shoes that pinched my toes but looked elegant when I stood at his side. The blouses in soft pastels that never suited my skin but had earned a passing compliment.

As I held each item, I felt the weight of compromise. It wasn't just fabric. It was memory. It was evidence of how often I had bent myself into shapes I thought would keep me loved. Every time I folded one into the vinnies bag, my stomach tightened. It felt terrifying - like I was stripping away layers of identity. But alongside the fear was something else: relief. With each hanger emptied, I felt the faintest echo of lightness. A sliver of space reclaimed. A corner of my life returned to me.

Then came the experimenting. At first, it felt clumsy, almost childlike. I tried on colours I had once avoided, shades I had convinced myself didn't belong to me. Bright reds, earthy greens, deep purples. I reached for fabrics that felt playful against my skin - flowing cotton, bold silks, soft knits that made me want to curl into myself. Some days, I laughed out loud in the mirror at the ridiculousness of it all - too loud, too much, too strange. But other days, I caught a glimpse of her. The woman I thought I had lost. The spark in my eye when I saw myself reflected not as a partner, not as a mother, not as anyone's anything - just as me.

And the whisper came: There she is

And then came my hair. Oh, my hair. For years, I had kept it blonde because that's who I'd become. Every time I sat in the salon chair, I swallowed the tug in my chest, the voice that whispered, this isn't you. I told myself it looked good. I told myself it suited me. But in truth, every strand felt like a lie I had chosen to tell.

I missed the richness of my natural brown - the depth of it, the warmth of it, the way it made me feel grounded, like myself. After the breakup, I caught my reflection one morning and felt a jolt of recognition, and not the good kind. My hair was bright and golden, my wardrobe filled with clothes chosen for someone else, and my eyes looked dulled by years of compromise. I stared at the mirror and thought, who is she? Because I don't know her anymore.

That was the day I decided: no more.

I went back to my natural hair colour. I still remember the first time I saw it in the mirror after the colour change, the way my reflection looked back at me with a familiarity that nearly brought me to tears. It was like greeting an old friend I hadn't seen in years, someone I had missed without even realising it.

It wasn't just hair. It was reclamation. It was proof that even the simplest choice could become a declaration: This is me. This crown is mine. From there, I began to rebuild through rituals. Little things at first. I lit candles in the morning, not for anyone else, but because the soft glow soothed me. I brewed coffee slowly, letting the steam rise and curl like a meditation. I read poetry before bed, words that reminded me of beauty, of rhythm, of life outside of heartbreak.

Each ritual became a rhythm, a heartbeat of my days. They weren't grand or dramatic. But they were mine. And then, slowly, I began reclaiming my dreams. I wrote down the goals I had shelved because they didn't fit into "us." Trips I had longed to take but postponed. Projects I had tucked into drawers because they didn't align with his vision. Even the versions of myself I had put on pause. The adventurous one, the creative one, the bold one.

Page by page, I began choosing them back.

It was terrifying at times. To admit that I wanted more. To dream again without knowing how it would all unfold. But it was also exhilarating. Like oxygen returning to lungs that had been starved. Every choice was a brushstroke. Every act was a jewel returned to my crown. And with each one, I felt the weight shift. Not the crushing weight of expectations or compromise, but the grounded, steady weight of authenticity.

The more I rebuilt, the more I realised: I hadn't been lost. I had been waiting.

STORIES OF REBUILDING

One friend told me that after her break-up, she signed up for a pottery class. She had never worked with clay before, but something about the idea of shaping and moulding with her hands called to her. "I wasn't any good," she laughed as she showed me the small bowls and lopsided cups she had kept. "But it wasn't about being good. It was about remembering what it felt like to create something from nothing, to touch the earth with my bare hands and watch it slowly become something."

She said that at first, the clay felt stubborn, heavy, unwilling to move. But the more she pressed, the more it softened, as if it too was learning to trust her again. And she realised that this was a reflection of her own heart. Hardened by loss, resistant at first, but softening little by little as she allowed herself to try, to feel, to create.

Another friend started hiking. She had never been what you'd call "outdoorsy," but the stillness of the trails drew her in after the chaos of separation. She said that at first, it was just about movement - putting one foot in front of the other, getting out of the house. But as the miles stretched behind her, she began to notice the quiet. The crunch of gravel beneath her shoes. The way the trees seemed to whisper in the breeze. She told me that in those moments, she heard her own voice more clearly than she had in years. Not the voice shaped by someone else's expectations, not the voice silenced by arguments or compromise, but her voice. The one that had been buried deep. She said, "It was as if the trail listened without judgment. And in that listening, I began to remember who I was."

Another friend found her way back to herself through writing. Not polished essays, not beautifully structured sentences - just raw, messy words scrawled onto paper. Some entries were angry, filled with scribbles that nearly tore through the page. Others were grief-stricken, ink blurred by tears. And some were only fragments: a single word, a question, a phrase like I survived today.

She told me, "It wasn't about writing well. It wasn't about anyone reading it. It was about giving myself a voice again. Hearing myself, without apology, without editing, without shrinking."

Her writing became her mirror, one that reflected truth without distortion.

And I could see, in each of their stories, a common thread: rebuilding doesn't always look like reinvention. It doesn't require you to pack up your life, move across the country, or suddenly become someone else. It is quieter than that, simpler than that.

It is choice. Small, consistent choices. Pottery bowls that wobble on their bases. Trails that leave your legs aching but your heart a little lighter. Pages filled with words that may never make sense to anyone else but are a lifeline to you.

Each choice whispers the same reminder: I am still here. I am not gone. I am returning to myself.

And maybe for you, it won't be pottery, or hiking, or writing. Maybe it will be painting your nails a colour you've always loved but never worn. Maybe it will be singing in the shower, even if your voice cracks. Maybe it will be planting herbs in small pots on your windowsill and watching them grow.

Whatever it is, it doesn't have to be grand. It doesn't have to be perfect. It doesn't even have to make sense to anyone else. It only has to remind you of yourself - the self that heartbreak could never take away.

Because every small act of rebuilding is not just a step forward. It is a jewel returned to your crown.

THE ARTIST METAPHOR

Rebuilding yourself is like painting a self-portrait.

At first, the canvas intimidates you. You stand before it blank, overwhelmed, afraid of making a mistake. But then you take up the brush. You make one stroke. Then another. Some strokes are messy. Some don't belong. Some are painted over. But gradually, the image begins to emerge.

And the woman staring back at you is not a stranger. She is you - fuller, freer, more radiant than ever.

Your crown gleams not because it is new, but because it now reflects resilience.

PRACTICES FOR REBUILDING

The Wardrobe Ritual

Stand in front of your clothes. Hold each piece and ask: Does this feel like me, or like someone else? Keep only what honours your crown.

The Hair Mirror

Ask yourself: does my hair reflect me, or someone else's preference? If not, change it. Your hair is not trivial! It is identity, expression, reclamation.

The Daily Choice

Each day, make one choice purely because it brings you joy. A song, a scent, a walk, a flavour. These small acts stack into identity.

The Dream List

Write 20 dreams that belong only to you. Don't censor. Circle one and take a small step toward it this week.

The Self-Portrait Journal

> *Describe yourself in words as if you were a character in a novel. Focus not on roles, but on essence. Who walks into the room? What energy does she carry? What crown does she wear?*

ASK YOURSELF

Where do you feel like a stranger in your own life?

What choices are you still making for someone else's approval?

What's one small choice today that could be a brushstroke of your true self? If you changed your outer appearance (clothes, hair, style) to reflect only you, what would it look like?

CHOOSING YOURSELF AGAIN

Rebuilding the self, you thought you lost isn't about reinvention. It's not about becoming someone entirely new or erasing the chapters that brought you here. It's about reclamation. It's about reaching back through the fog of heartbreak, disappointment, and expectation, and choosing yourself again - piece by piece, moment by moment.

It's about looking at the fragments scattered across the floor and realising they were never rubbish. They were never the remains of a broken life. They were always pieces of you, waiting to be honoured, waiting to be gathered and placed back where they belong.

It is not a single, triumphant decision. It is thousands of tiny ones.

Choosing clothes that reflect who you are, not who someone else wanted you to be. Choosing rituals that nourish you, not performative habits meant to impress. Choosing passions that light you up, even if no one else understands them. Choosing dreams that belong to you alone, not borrowed visions handed down by family, partners, or society. For me, reclamation looked like going back to my natural hair colour. It may sound small, even trivial, but for me it was monumental. Every blonde strand had been a compromise, a silent agreement to please someone else. Returning to brown was like greeting an old friend - a version of myself who had always been there, waiting, patient, unwavering.

For you, reclamation may look different. It may be the way you move your body, the music you choose to play, the career path you decide to follow, the city you decide to live in. It might be as subtle as the fragrance you spray on your body before you walk out the door, or as bold as starting a brand new chapter of your life altogether.

But the message is the same: *I am still here. I am choosing me.*

Every choice you make - no matter how small - is a brushstroke on the canvas of your identity. Some strokes are bold, sweeping, defiant. Others are delicate, quiet, almost invisible to anyone but you. But together, they form a picture that is unmistakably yours.

And as you rebuild, you begin to see something profound: you were never truly lost. You were never erased. You were never gone. What you thought had disappeared was only hidden, waiting for you to choose differently.

You were waiting; patiently, powerfully, quietly - for yourself to come home.

And when you do, when you step into that reclamation fully, life itself begins to shift. Doors open. Opportunities appear. Joy bubbles up in unexpected places. Relationships deepen. Strangers smile at you differently. The world notices when you wear your crown.

From this place of reclamation, you are ready for what comes next: stepping into abundance. Because abundance does not arrive when you chase it or demand it. Abundance arrives when you align with your truth.

When you wear your crown as your true self... not tilted, not hidden, not borrowed. That's when life responds.

"The moment you remember your worth,

life remembers you too."

10

ABUNDANCE UNFOLDING

THE FIRST SIGNS

I remember the first time I felt abundance unfolding after heartbreak. It wasn't dramatic. It wasn't the kind of cinematic breakthrough you'd expect in a movie - no cheque in the mail, no sudden windfall, no grand romantic gesture sweeping me off my feet.

It was something small.

I was standing at the beach one morning, a coffee warming my hands, the waves crashing gently against the sand. For the first time in months, I wasn't crying. I wasn't analysing, replaying, or aching. I was simply standing there, watching the sunrise bleed into the horizon, when I realised, I was smiling.

The smile caught me off guard. It wasn't painted on for anyone else. It wasn't forced. It rose up naturally, like a tide I hadn't felt in months.

And in that quiet moment, I realised: this was abundance.

Not the money in a bank account. Not the titles or achievements. Not the glitter of material success. Abundance was joy. And not even loud joy - not the kind that demands attention or shouts across a room. This was the quiet, golden kind. The kind that wells up from the inside, subtle but steady, filling you until you overflow.

From that moment, I began to notice more. A stranger holding a door open for me. An old song coming on the radio that reminded me of a freer time. Unexpected laughter in conversations with friends that felt deeper, more nourishing, more real than before. Small opportunities at work that led to bigger ones.

It was as though the universe had been waiting for me to steady my crown before it could pour these gifts into my life.

What Abundance Really Means

Abundance is one of those words we hear all the time, usually attached to wealth, career milestones, or luxury lifestyles. But true abundance is far bigger, far richer, far more human than that.

Abundance is:

- The deep breath that fills your lungs when you pause long enough to notice the miracle of being alive.

- The laugh that bubbles up unexpectedly, reminding you that lightness still exists.

- The silence that feels peaceful instead of lonely.

- The opportunities that arrive not because you chased them, but because you opened yourself to them.

- The relationships that deepen because you dared to show up as your real, unpolished self.

- The flow of resources - financial, emotional, creative - that comes when you stop gripping control and allow life to surprise you.

Abundance isn't about what you collect. It's about what you allow.

It's not measured in possessions.

It's measured in presence.

MY OWN STORY OF ABUNDANCE

My days began to fill with small serendipities, chance encounters with people who inspired me, conversations that lifted me, opportunities that seemed to arrive out of nowhere. There was laughter too - bubbling up unexpectedly, catching me off guard in the best way.

I remember thinking: I thought I'd lost everything. Instead, I found myself. And once I found myself, life began to find me.

After months of slowly rebuilding, I started noticing subtle but powerful shifts in my own life. Business opportunities appeared that had once been closed off to me, doors I thought were locked forever seemed to ease open. New friendships blossomed - deeper, kinder, genuine.

And it wasn't just the big things. Even the smallest moments began to feel significant - my favourite café seat waiting for me as if it had been reserved, the unexpected kindness of a stranger's compliment, the warmth of the sun on my face on a day I had braced myself for heaviness. Each one felt like evidence. Proof that life itself was whispering: Yes. More of this.

What struck me most was that none of it appeared when I was striving, proving, or clinging. It only began when I loosened my grip. When I stopped performing and started breathing. When I carried my crown not as an act, but as truth.

That was the lesson: abundance isn't chased. It unfolds.

STORIES OF OTHERS

A friend shared how she had spent years hiding her art, afraid of criticism. She apologised constantly - for her ideas, for her talent, for her existence. But the moment she stopped apologising, the moment she stood tall in her truth, something shifted. People began noticing her work. Her paintings started selling. She told me, "It wasn't that my art changed. It was that I changed."

Her story reminded me: abundance doesn't require force. It requires authenticity.

THE GARDEN METAPHOR

Think of your life as a garden. When heartbreak hits, the garden feels bare. The soil is cracked, the flowers wilt, and no matter where you look, nothing seems to grow. You walk through it and think: this place is dead.

But gardens don't stay bare forever. When you begin to heal, you are tending the soil again. You water it with truth. You plant seeds of joy. You nurture yourself with patience.

And then, quietly, almost without fanfare, green shoots appear. Buds bloom. Fruit ripens. *Slowly, steadily, abundantly.*

Abundance is not sudden magic. It is the natural unfolding of a tended garden.

PRACTICES FOR ABUNDANCE

Gratitude Journal

Each night, write down three things you are grateful for. Not grand gestures, small, ordinary moments. Gratitude expands what you notice.

Abundance Visualisation

Close your eyes. Picture yourself wearing your crown, surrounded by the love, opportunities, and joy you desire. Imagine how it feels. Carry that feeling with you throughout your day.

Generosity Practice

Give something freely each day; a compliment, a smile, a kind message, a small act of service. Abundance multiplies when it flows.

The Crown Affirmations

Whisper to yourself daily:

- *I am open to abundance*

- *My crown attracts what aligns with me. Joy, love, and wealth flow easily to me.*

ASK YOURSELF

Where in your life have you already seen abundance unfolding? What seeds do you want to plant in your garden now?

How does your energy shift when you wear your crown with confidence? What daily practices help you notice abundance instead of scarcity?

THE CROWN THAT RADIATES

Abundance isn't about waiting for life to change. It's about remembering your crown and living in alignment with it. When you do, life responds. Joy bubbles up. Opportunities appear. Relationships deepen. Resources flow.

The crown was never lost. It was always yours. And when you wear it steadily, abundance unfolds. Not because you chase it, but because you are finally open to receiving it.

This is the closing truth of your journey: the crown was always yours. It may have slipped, it may have felt heavy, it may have been forgotten - but it never left. And now, you wear it not only for yourself, but for the world that is drawn to its light.

"You were never broken, only buried beneath the noise of who the world told you to be.

The moment you remember, life begins to rearrange itself in your favour.

Because the truth is, you were never becoming - you were only ever remembering.

And when you finally rise into that truth, your world will expand in ways you once thought impossible.

This is where remembering ends... and becoming begins... this time, as the woman you were always meant to be."

11

THE CROWN WAS ALWAYS YOURS

COMING FULL CIRCLE

When I began this journey, I thought I had lost everything. Heartbreak had shattered my illusions. Expectations weighed heavy on my shoulders. The mirrors I had relied on for so long lay in pieces, leaving me unable to recognise the woman staring back at me. I thought my crown had slipped so far that I would never find it again - that I was destined to walk through life alone, unseen, unworthy.

But here is the truth that revealed itself slowly, quietly, insistently: the crown was never gone.

It had slipped, yes. It had felt unbearably heavy at times. It had been buried beneath layers of grief, expectations, compromises, and distorted reflections. But it had never left me. It had always been here - steady, patient, waiting for me to remember.

And this is the truth I want you to carry with you as you close these pages:

your crown was never lost either.

It may have slipped. It may have felt heavy. It may have been buried under years of trying to please, of bending, of surviving. But it has never, not once, left you. Your crown is here. Always was. Always will be.

THE CROWN THROUGH EVERY CHAPTER

This journey has taken us through heartbreak and loss, through shattered mirrors and broken expectations. And yet, through it all, the crown remained.

In heartbreak, we learnt that pain creates fog but not fact. The crown remained. Under expectations, we discovered that not every crown handed to you was yours to wear.

In shattered mirrors, we learnt that you cannot outsource your worth to someone else's gaze.

In picking up the pieces, we saw that healing is a mosaic built from small, daily acts.

Through the crown within, we reconnected with the compass of your soul, steady and unshakable.

In detachment, we learnt to lift the crown lightly, holding life with open hands. Through quiet luxury, we embodied elegance, dignity, and presence.

In rebuilding, you chose yourself again, brushstroke by brushstroke and in abundance, we saw that when you wear your crown with confidence, life responds with joy, opportunities, and love.

Every step was a reminder. Every chapter was a return. Every metaphor was a path back to yourself.

The Crown Ritual

I want to leave you with one final ritual, a way to anchor this truth so that no matter how loud the world becomes, you can always return to it.

1. Find a quiet place.

2. Close your eyes.

3. Picture a crown hovering just above your head - glowing, steady, radiant.

4. Slowly, gently, lower it onto your head. Feel its weight, not as a burden, but as presence.

5. Whisper to yourself: This crown was always mine. I wear it now, every day, with grace and strength.

Do this whenever you feel lost, unseen, or weighed down. The ritual isn't about imagining something new. It's about remembering what was always there.

12

A MESSAGE FROM PAMELA

As you turn the final page, know this: you are not walking away empty-handed. You are walking away crowned.

Your journey will not always be easy. There will be days when the crown feels tilted again, when grief fogs your vision, when old lies try to creep back in. But you now have the tools. You now have the knowing. You now have the remembrance.

The crown was never lost.

Not in heartbreak. Not in rejection. Not in silence. Not in any of the storms you have weathered.

And as you lift your head today, wearing it once more, you are stepping into something far greater than survival. You are stepping into sovereignty. Into presence. Into the kind of radiance that doesn't just transform your life but quietly shifts the lives of everyone around you.

This is not the end. This is a beginning.

Because the truth of crowns is that they are never truly just for us. When you wear yours, steady and strong, you remind every woman around you that she has one too. You become a mirror, not the distorted kind that breaks under pressure, but a true mirror; one that reflects worth, dignity, and light.

So, wear it, every day. Wear it when you rise. Wear it when you stumble. Wear it when you laugh, when you cry, when you love, when you walk into rooms that once intimidated you. Wear it in silence. Wear it in celebration. Wear it as the reminder that you are whole.

And if ever you forget, if ever the fog rolls in again, just do your best and return to these words.

Return to the ritual. Return to yourself.

Because the crown was always yours.

It always will be.

And the world is waiting to see you wear it.

ACKNOWLEDGEMENT

To my children - my greatest teachers, my reason, and my reminder that love and resilience can rewrite any story.

To my family and friends – thank you for standing beside me in the seasons of both silence and celebration - your belief in me held me up when I forgot how to stand.

To the men I have loved - thank you for shaping chapters of my story. Through joy and heartbreak, you gave me the lessons that forced me to grow.

To the women who will read these words - you are the heartbeat of this work. Every page was written with you in mind, in the hope that you see your own strength reflected back at you.

And finally, to the quiet mornings, the ocean, the sunrise, and the universe itself - thank you for whispering guidance when I needed it most.

About the Author

Pamela Blaney is an author and entrepreneur who helps women rediscover their worth and reclaim their confidence. With a background in social psychology and more than 20 years of experience, Pamela blends academic insight with lived experience, writing from the powerful intersection of psychology and spirituality: where emotional healing becomes true transformation.

Her debut book, The Crown You Never Lost, was born from her own journey through heartbreak, rebuilding, and the profound moment she realised she was never broken. Through a fusion of psychology, intuitive guidance, and raw, honest storytelling, Pamela reminds every woman that her crown: her dignity, confidence, and self-worth, was never lost, only forgotten.

Living on the Sunshine Coast of Australia, Pamela draws inspiration from the ocean, the sunrise, and her most cherished role: being a mother. She continues to write, design digital education experiences, and build platforms that support women around the world in reclaiming their inner strength.

Her words create a safe space for readers to pause, reconnect with their feminine energy, and rise with clarity, resilience, and quiet elegance.

Alongside her writing, Pamela is the founder of Eshora: a lifestyle empowerment brand born from starting again. Grounded in psychology, energy, and intentional design, Eshora helps individuals understand themselves, uncover their purpose, identify their niche, and guides them to transform it into a lasting legacy.

Connect with Pamela: ESHORA.COM.AU

www.ingramcontent.com/pod-product-compliance
Lightning Source LLC
Chambersburg PA
CBHW071248070526
44583CB00017B/2371